MW00575138

MOMENTARY ORDINARY

For my friends,
Joann and harry!
Hope you enjoy
these words.

Marilyn 3. Wendan

Pebblebrook Press

an imprint of *Stoneboat*—www.stoneboatwi.com.

Acknowledgments

I would like to thank the following for first publishing these poems:

Finishing Line Press chapbook *Adventures in Paradise*: "Roundabout"

Making It Speak: Poets & Artists in Cahoots: "Iditarod"

The Midwest Prairie Review Journal: "Hospitality"

Red Cedar Review: "Kabuki"

Stoneboat: "In Chicago" and "Something"

Verse Wisconsin: "S. of Vernon, Indiana, State Hwy 7" and "True Grit"

Wisconsin Fellowship of Poets Calendar: "A Winter Walk to School"

Wisconsin Fellowship of Poets Museletter: "Morning Tidbits at the Post Office" and "Unicorn"

www.yourdailypoem.com: "Trick or Treat"

Many thanks also to my family and to Georgia Ressmeyer, Marilyn L. Taylor, Rob Pockat, Signe Jorgenson, Lisa Vihos, and Jim Giese.

→ Indicates no stanza break

Dedicated to my husband Tom
for his honesty and loving support

Momentary Ordinary ©2014 by Pebblebrook Press, an imprint of
Stoneboat. Editors: Jim Giese, Signe Jorgenson, Rob Pockat, Lisa Vihos.
Cover art: Marilyn Zelke-Windau. *View* ©2014. All sketches also by
Marilyn Zelke-Windau. Author photograph by Tom Windau.
ISBN: 978-0692331439

Table of Contents

Momentary Ordinary

What Nana Knows

A Strange Transport

ON THE FRONT PORCH

Morning Tidbits at the Post Office

"May I help you?"
offered the uniformed clerk at the counter.

"I'd like to send this package,"
replied the woman,
holding out a pink, paper-covered carton.

"Parcel post to Seattle?"

"No, express mail please. She needs it now!"

"Are the contents breakable, hazardous,
liquid, or perishable?"

"No. It's an extra large size shirt for my daughter.
I'm to have a granddaughter, in just three months."

"Well, how nice. And what's her name going to be?"

The short, plain woman straightened taller.
"Zoe Alexis, I'm pleased to tell," she voiced a bit louder,
"named after both her nanas."

The line of small town ears perked up, stored chatter tidbits.

The Promise of Greens

He came in for a haircut.
It had been a while.
I think he'd grown two inches since.
His hair: long, straight,
oily with lard leftover
from morning toast before school.
My scissors murmured, "Help!"

He paid with promises of greens
and berries, black and blue,
after the 2 bits he offered
was found wanting.
His jean cuffs dragged hair out the door:
nest-makings for summer songbirds,
worthy recipients.

I went home midday for dinner.
Martha snipped,
"When you gonna mow the lawn?
It's ferocious!"

I looked out
over my red beans and rice,
a little chicken,
then hush-puppied a reply.

The side-yard view
showed that one promise of greens
had been fulfilled.
Yellow-green, blue-green,
dark green, light green.
Not broad-leafed like kale,
collards, mustard.
This was chive-hair grass.

This was like his hair,
grown two inches since.
Long, straight,
leftover from many mornings.
Verdant, flopped-line waves
were queued up.
Take a number.
Make an appointment.
The mower murmured, "Help!"

Maldea and Cubitus

In the years I lived there, I noticed her many times.
Walking, always walking.
Trudging would perhaps be a better word.
Maldea trudged the streets of town methodically.

Weighting her left arm was a large, black, faux-leather purse.
It diamond-opened at the top.
Zipper broken, personals were exposed.
Worn at the corners, the bottom seam had been taped in duct silver.
The strap was belt-like.
The buckle tooth held at hole five.
The leftover length curled like a goose neck.

Cubitus, the pudgy dog who trailed behind her,
rhythmically lurched at that goose neck.
His old, cork-short legs and pull-along belly did not allow for
jumping.
He could smell the peanut butter crackers,
little pads of pug-dog pleasure.
A leash necklaced Maldea's ample right wrist.
It had no means of escape.

They were a pair, both squat in stature,
both fleshy, in need of brushing.
No groom.
They sweated the sidewalks together as distanced companions.
Their pattern of path repeated Broadway to Pine, Pine to Henry,
Henry to Leaven, Leaven back to Broadway.

Last Tuesday I saw her again down in town.
Same purse, less weight,
no leash.

Home Bees

There are about 436 bees
who have made their home
behind a panel of our hot tub.
They sift warm air as I sink
into 98-degree water.

I watch the jets make hemisphere-
bubbles on the surface.
In meditation, I lift my palms
upward, float them
like lotus blossoms,
rounded petals, not pointed.

I turn my hands over,
raise fingers
to two families of four.
If only I had a marker,
I could make their faces,
smiling, buoyant.

They swim in the currents,
in the wrinkled surface water.
They enjoy time together.
They are never separated.

A lone bee circles,
contemplates its sweet life.
I do, too.

Trio

Flora went into the garden room,
opened the cupboard door of the potting bench,
withdrew rooting hormone and a peat pot.
She filled it with soil.
White perlite lumps peppered its surface.
She dipped her finger into the nurture compound,
stuck it into the soil.
She grew two inches in an hour.

In the atrium, Celmira knelt
to touch the fountain's water.
A windy day, this, she could feel a spiral of breeze
funneling down from the openness above,
feel the spray of mist pellets
from the blossoming wet plume.
She put her tongue out to catch the drops.

Magdalene brought the torch in the evening,
tilted it to the trees on the wide lawns.
In an instant they were blaze candles
lighting a silhouette of the house.

Flora removed her finger from the soil.
Celmira swallowed.
Magdalena stared upward
as a circle of bees haloed the burning trees.

The Hairpin Ladies

Edna, Agnes, Myrtle and Mildred meet
for coffee and kuchen on Thursday mornings.
Children grown, husbands gone to work
or gone,
sheets and slips flap on sun lines.

Barn kittens fed,
cow milked,
chickens scattered like feed,
the ladies cylinder their tresses
around nape or crown,
zigzag-pinhold the ends.

They press scented hankies to throat,
finger them down bodices,
push-clip rhinestone earrings to lobes,
walk dustpaths to parlors,
alternating weekly.

Hugs and how d'ya do's
hasten cane chairs out from under table.
Grace begins the union of friends.
A hymn continues it after gossip-chat,
and kuchen smiles remind them
to sing a round before whisking crumbs
and clearing up cups.

Their to-home then hurried steps
dust-powder comforted shoes,
make dinner fulfilled.

Something

The man in the doorway smiles me away
as I take my leave
in a loud-mouthed muffler car.
He silently shouts, "Come back.
Stay with me. I have something
growing inside—something
me, but not. I couldn't tell you
I'm afraid."

It's a mass without benefit of incense.
It's one lump with no desire for two.
Outward appearance reveals nothing
of interior secrets:
a Bismarck, an entrée of cordon bleu,
a body.

There are those who jackknife out hernias,
those who are self operators:
soliloquy surgeons.
In the end, they too need orderlies,
assistance on this side.

I circle the block, curb and quiet exhaust.
We all need accompaniment
to play a last role, privately scripted.
Mortality dons a Janus mask
with two eyes closed.

Mayo Magic

"Hell, man, it's real!"

"How can it be real?" asked the man.

"It's made out of an egg, man.
It's an ochre blob birth hill.
An ant could trampoline jump it,
get swallowed in and never again
ricochet off into the agar puddle.
It's emulsified, dude!"

"Yeah, there's oil—
virgin amber that drips,
as a blender beats rhythm."

"But how come it's white, man?
It can't get white from yellow and clear and amber.
It starts real but something gets to it."

"It's air, man. Air."

"Nah, it's magic, man:
mayo magic."

The Sign Is Out

"I've got it here somewhere," he said,
in response to an inquiry
about a cast iron muffin pan.
"No, we're only open by appointment,
or when the sign is out.
I'm tired.
I cleared out Mom's stuff
when she died.
She gave us fair warning—
ovarian cancer,
said, 'This is valuable.
Look it up.
Price it.
Take it out of here.
I won't need it.
Your father wouldn't remember it,
that it was a wedding present.
It could fetch a nice price for you.'"

I bought the cast iron muffin pan.
It had been on my daughter's wish list for four years.
I had cleared out my mother's house
when she died, fair warning at age 93.
I knew the sentimental sorting.
I knew the emotional eviction.
I understood his longing to close his shop
in a year's time.

About Time

Two second-past-middle women sat in the house
one on the dawn side,
one on the dusk.

On settee edge sitting,
the twilight woman fidgeted anxiously,
"I haven't enough.
I've never had enough.
I'll never have enough.
Why can't I have more?
More will make it easier.
More will make it better.
More will make it right."

Ghost horses are iron-shoeing the interstate,
grey-like,
clomping the pavement,
gaining more power,
more distance,
winning.

Settled into her setting
horizontal eyes gazing east,
the second woman raised her lids to white
and waited.
"I have enough.
I've always had enough.
I'll always have enough.
I don't need more.
I don't want more.
More is more.

$\longrightarrow$

More is equal.
We are equal.
We have the same:
enough."

There are ants on the lawncloth
traveling at picneck speed
up the wrinkles
over the folds
down to the dark troughs where crumbs may await
across the townships, some red, some white
ever moving, determined onward.
Hiking the ridgeline
they stop only to lift up
their dead other, not recognizing themselves.

In the hallway of the house
a scream can be heard
and a burp
and a sigh
and a laugh.

The mirror in the hall
shows only one face,
one woman.
Time is not in long hand.
Time is not in short hand.
It is not in light or darkness.
It doesn't recognize itself.
Nor do I.

On the Front Porch

It was a day of errands,
a day of from here to there,
of deposit and pick up,
of chores, not visits.
Driving down Monroe Street
I passed your house.
It may have been your house
or it may have been your son's
or daughter's house.
At 25 miles per hour in the city,
it was a quick glance.
You were seated on the front porch,
a full-facing, windowed front porch.
Your hair was neat, cut short, prim.
You had on a dark cardigan sweater,
navy blue, I think, unbuttoned,
over a white Peter Pan collared blouse.
I couldn't see your hands.
I couldn't see your legs, your feet.
You were very still, gazing,
just gazing with a blank stare
at the outside world:
the world on Monroe Street.
Not much action on Monroe Street—
only cars passing, no pedestrians,
no school children at 11:00 a.m. on a Thursday.
My thoughts of chores and errands paused.
You stayed.
You stayed on that porch with your quietness.
Your vacant look echoed my day
through Target, the bank drive-up window,

$\longrightarrow$

Piggly Wiggly, and the post office.
I deliberately retraced my route
on the way home.
Your world had broadened
because you weren't there.
Mine had narrowed
because for me you still were.

Bird Mother

You're angry. I know.
You built your house here.
You liked the quiet of the neighborhood.
No one out and about.
It seemed a nice place to move in,
a nice place to raise children.
That was when it was 40 degrees
and threatening snow.
You must have taken an early flight north.

I hung the spring-flowered wreath
on the side porch, the north side,
where the thermometer is.
I was hopeful.
Channel 12 news kept saying,
"Chance of snow."

You thought the wreath was inviting.
You brought your own décor to it:
mud, twigs, and best of all,
a length of white, curlable gift ribbon.
You're quite the weaver.
I'm impressed.
It's not overshot, or twill,
or even tabby.
It's more like lace weave,
given the white, curlable gift ribbon.

Now that there are three
blue eggs in your house,
you think you own the neighborhood.
I'm a mother, too.
I understand protection.

→

I understand warmth and hovering.
I know you have a job to do.
Your work is cut out for you.
Night and day, sitting,
except for a few excursions out to eat.

I have a job to do, too.
The hostas at the foot of the porch
need weeding and mulch.
I can't help it.
I have to be here.
I have to do it.

You can chirp all you want.
Take a break.
Go out to eat early.
I'll be out of here soon.
I'm not touching those eggs.
I'm not walking the porch.
I'm not even looking you in the eye,
except slyly, peripherally.

Get used to it.
I'm going to be out here.
I'm going to be around.
Think of me as Grandma.
I'll tell them stories
while they're waiting
for worms,
while they're waiting
to fly.

ALL
THE ROADS

All the Roads

The pages of Rand McNally open
to line colors: black
dashes for gravel,
blue continuous for supers, red
for ones less traveled, green
for pay as you go.

All the roads have destinations,
whether to riverbanks,
mountain highlights,
farm fields,
mini burgs,
major majors,
capitals, or
country casualties.

Empty circles and poured black dots
delineate importance
of populated areas,
which are caught
in active blue and green lines
like spiders' webs,
or are afterthoughts to the right of red,
or black-blinded
in the dashing of hopes
off the highway.

All roads connect.
All roads lead to,
and away.
The present is passed
via white lines on the left,
or, rightly, on the shoulders
of those who are impatiently driven
to continue.

Everything's OK

He slid hot scrambled eggs
into a plastic square covered pan,
explained that the circular
forms in the other pan
were egg, sausage and cheese,
baked in a muffin pan.
He wiped Fruit Loops, All Bran
and Cheerios residue from the counter.
"Everything OK? Taste OK?"

We all sat at little tables
in the breakfast room of the motel,
making gluttonous decisions about waffles,
gravy and biscuits, peanut butter toast.
Each of us had contributed to the emptiness
of the fresh fruit bowl.
No orange, apple or banana was left.
These fruits travel,
and we were, after all,
travelers.

"My Grandma taught me well. She had
a restaurant, more like a drive-in
off-the-road diner.
I was her main help when I was little.
I cleaned counters. I filled bowls,
jars. I bussed dishes, washed them, too.
I moved up to head short-order cook.
That was when I was 17. I'm 43 now.
She's 92, still in her right head.
I had a heart attack, surgery,
had to take it easy for some time.
Now I'm here, and back in my element.
Everything OK? Taste good?"

Oh, Pa

"Oh, Pa," she said
when she saw that he was ready to go.
It was a Friday, 10:30 in the morning.
He looked so debonair:
white shirt, blue pants,
white shining shoes,
white hat, white hair.

She went upstairs to their small room
on the west side of Milwaukee,
changed her spring green selection
to a blue shirt, white flared pants,
blue leather strappy sandals
and a white, floppy sun hat
to cover her ivory-white curls.

A strong, new summer day,
full blown with hot light,
a whispered breeze.
She knew he remembered that climate
of his homeland.
In step, they left the cerulean car
on the asphalt of the state fair parking lot
and walked, he in front,
she trailing just a little,
in deference, in respect for the day.

They color-matched their flag of origin,
stepped proudly to their Greek festival,
thought of the day's vote
of a proud, independent, scholarly nation
stabbed by modern times,
corrupted brutally by greed.

His handkerchief at the ready,
triangling from his side pocket,
asked for, joyously shouted
for the dance.
"Opa!" he bellowed with pride,
gratitude and remembrance
as his bloodbeat and the bouzouki began.

Bus Ride

Abercrombie left home,
bought a ticket on the outbound Greyhound,
climbed aboard,
decided the seat next to the little redhead looked fine.
Eventually he leaned in with a "Howdy there, Miss."

"Finally I get a live one,"
Gertie thought as she
hoisted her bosom up from her belt.
"If I didn't know better, I'd think he
just sat down here to make eyes at me."

"Kellogg's my name: Abercrombie Kellogg.
Looks as though we'll be gettin' in to
Memphis at three.
Nashville at noon.
Opryland Hotel's in Nashville.
Perhaps you'd care to take lunch with me."

(Quiet, little heart. Don't scare this one off.)

"Really, sir, that's very kind of you to offer.
Since I am all alone on this journey,
thankful I'd surely be to join you."

Unbeknownst to her,
victim of first-sight love,
wishes turn to
xxxes and
yes becomes the answer to
zephyrs wafting westward.

Disharmony

His face was death grey,
jowled in silence
while guttural sounds
of an ancient flute called.
He played his accordion
to the Croatian norm.
His demeanor belied heritage.
The fast paced, frenetic
goulash of sound
awakened the cimbalom
pounding of heartbeats
now from Cleveland,
once Zagreb.
Never to be back home again
took its toll, reverberated
in audience foot pounding.
A waist-scarved singer
starved out notes
gypsies had borrowed
century nights before.

Kabuki

She sat to the left of the stage house,
her garments as stiff as her right-angle posture,
white, her face, with sharp-raised eyebrows,
hair drawn back, up, in smoothed
lacquer-black waves.

Simple room with mat and table.
A lone flower in raku vase.
Paper-screen walls, sliding the silence,
awaiting the brother, the grandfather, priest.

Only the tea came,
green and frothy.

The koto bewailed
her emotionless face.

Fan moving cautiously,
while catching her footsteps
she whined a song—
sing song—
of fate.

Mirror Image

1.

His hot feet tread firmly. The hill soil was hard packed,
not sandy slippage. Dry though, very dry.
The sun had worked hard over centuries to make it so.
Others' step rhythms had helped maintain the path.

The air burned his inhales and gave his exhales time constraints.
Those short puffs rid his lungs of moisture. Thirst was mind-evident.

Taking care to look in a circular pattern, as dogs do before lying down,
he saw no snakes, no scorpions, no ants. Safe to sit, he did so.
He stared at the sun glare, the treeless landscape,
then narrowed his gaze to the continuous yellow ochre earth.

From his shoulder-slung bag, Tomas withdrew a skin pouch of water,
now only partially full. He drank two measured gulps, capped it with care
and replaced it after pressing it once to his forehead.

Closing his dry eyes, he thought of that second of coolness,
of water's relief—a relief where rivers flow and lakes
puddle the landscape. That image had come to him many times.
It was a dream place that brought a comfort, a settled recognition,
a knowing.

2.

Sliding the mud-slippery grassed path to the pond, Tom knew
from the squelching that his socks, as well as his hiking boots,
were soaked through. His nose dripped like a downspout and
runoff from his curly hair pattered his collarbones.

Gazing down, Tom saw his reflection silvered in the surface
of the water. The moon had risen full after the storm.

Frogs were caterwauling in delight. No need for a dip yet,
their skin was rain-shimmered. The cool front breeze sent
a shiver through him and a loud sneeze caught him by surprise.
It spewed moist beads to the already swollen pond. He wished
he had worn a better jacket—a slicker. Warmth escaped his wet
insulation.

Looking up at the moon, he conjured again visions of wafting waves of heat,
dry heat, hot sun, parch-cracked soil and only a sky of blueness. That earth
beneath him was home, a part of him that seemed to have existed within him
long before he was born, not this wet world.

Robert Burns

She can't remember his words
until she sings them:
the melodies of her youth,
others' youth, and of old age
in Scotland, of Scotland.
She says he was a rogue.
He loved women,
not just one, or many—
"and aye, he did!"—
but the idea of,
the being of women.
He left them with verse
and with children.
His poems became songs,
songs to bring memories.
Written with repetition,
in a language
that gathers in the cheek,
rolls off the tongue,
reverberates in its rhythm,
and echoes now
in her voice.

Shaping Figures

She stood with her arms akimbo.
I couldn't see her face.
Sitting at the café, the sun behind me
flashed blind her visage.
A triangle world was revealed
via skinny flesh frame.

There, the swollen sea
welted blue black mounds
to the shore.

There, the parallel planks
of boardwalk clicked echoes
of sandals' pine-arched soles.

There, the pinks of knees,
the corals of cheeks,
the magentas of mantles
of bikini flesh were sun hued.

She gestured. The shape changed.
The triangle morphed
into a narrow rectangle.
Through it, a thin ray of light
back-flashed, brought eye-tears,
and I turned away
to the circle rim of my glass.

Masai Boy's Song

There's a hollow bass tone
in the voice of the young Masai boy.
Open mouthed, he mimics the sun,
the full moon.
He sings the African earth,
sings the mound of termite mothers,
sings the sacred life of cows.
His voice no one of his people hears.
Only he and the wind hear.
The listening breeze
dances the red clay soil.
Her beads vibrate
a hip chest song,
call on him repeatedly
to begin his song again.

Hospitality

There's a woman from Romania
who daily cleans a room, several,
at a sunshiny resort for those
who do not worry about regular,
or decaf coffee packets,
sugars, creamers,
red plastic cylindrical sticks,
snow-forgotten bleached towels,
shampoo/conditioner
in coconut mango combos,
facial moisturizers, aloe-infused,
ice makers providing percussion
in the afternoon, between drinks,
between naps.

Yusmila does the worrying
for her rooms, their clients,
and her family waiting
for wired money.
She cares more for her green
card, her green send-ons
than the resort's green label.
Never met, name on a card
of welcome, of urgency, need,
never mind, never to be known,
Yusmila shakes pillows,
tosses them like her dreams
into the air.

South of Vernon, Indiana, State Highway 7

A small, square, wooden table had been set
on newly-shooting dandelions and bluegrass.
The wind picked up a lacy corner of the tea cloth,
triangling it.
A small lamp atop.
One cup and saucer.
No chairs for invitees.
Surrounding it, rusted trailers were parked
like chess men,
boxing the table in check.
Across the state highway,
a house with moldy green shingles
had collapsed—
karate-chopped once
in the spine of its roofline.
Teatime was over.
We motored past
with blinders of quiet solitude.

Tantatted Tooth

I hold between my fingers
a molar, extracted from the jaw
of an ancient aardvark.
It is pitted on its biting surface
from years of grinding the narrow,
knobby branches of the tantat tree.
Its base "V" arrows downward,
exposed now,
when before, it held true
to its gummy tissue,
its moist jaw home,
its mouth of earnest eating.
The aardvark tooth is stone,
striated grey and yellow-beige.
Evidence of sugar shows:
sparkles which glint the sun's midday rays
in celebration of time, of strength, of endurance.

The Watch

Sally Pearl has a beauty salon and boutique
on a sidewalkless street in Alabama.
She waits for her nine o'clock late cut-and-color,
watches sun glare the kudzu on her front-lawn elm.

Louis Taranto has a cracked stucco seafood store
with a tin roof and shrimp, fish, oysters
in Florida's panhandle.
He paces the wood aisle, anxious at seven
for the freezer repairman
before opening the door to morning customers.

Max Berne press-clasps a padlock tight
next to eleven others
on a Brooklyn Bridge twisted cable
on the dark anniversary evening
of his late wife's birthday.

I look at my wrist.
The watch there keeps good the forty years I've spent
since receiving it as a seventeen-year-old in Illinois:
a gift from now-dead parents,
its face glommed on by three infants
mouthing the second hand,
filing first teeth on the side-winder.

Plastic discs once pressed the circle,
rotated to acknowledge the standard of hours
in Chicago, New York, Berlin.

I think of the waste of one moment,
the time that continues unabated,

$\rightarrow$

continues without Sally's or Louis's or my consent,
continues without any defense mounted,
any armor or fort or wall constructed to protect,
to keep time from overcoming, overwhelming.

I free my wrist, put the watch in the drawer,
let it tick there with me deaf
until we all forget about time.

In Brazil today

a woman
was struck down by a car

I walk
I am walking
down this road
to my village

my cinta
it is tight

tears follow my feet

Emptying Space

I was amazed. She agreed to move
up north here to my hunting cabin.

West Allis. Yes, she had surgery—
breast cancer in 2005.

Decorated the cabin with flowers,
planted garden, whistled while doing dishes.
My hunting buddies were in awe—
never saw a female transition so well.

I have three recliners, a bed, a wheel chair,
many other things.

No, I don't want to run an ad.
My son is bringing me a pool table.
I have to make room.

I'm giving these plants to my bartender.
There's a Christmas cactus, blooming now late.
African violets, their plump, fuzzy leaves thin,
an iron cross plant still red-leaved in hope.

I have a trailer. If you want the recliners,
I can bring them to you.
I'm giving them away for free.

Those are Laddy's dog toys
littered all over the living room.
He growls a lot now.

That piano was here when I bought the place.
It's kind of a fixture.
She liked to play.

Her bed is still there all made.

I'll help you carry the recliner to your car.

In a Costa Rican Salon

Have you seen the toes of a sloth?
Have you seen those toenails?
Revlon, OPI, all colorists are calling
with "let me at them" envious cries,
with designs hitherto unknown—
orchid patterns, ant marches,
croton and philodendron overlaps,
motivated solely by sloth points.
These clawed wonders take their time
pulling the door open,
admitting to appointments,
hanging up their coats,
themselves,
accepting hot towels, paw massage.
Manicurists find they are out on a limb
making small talk with these customers.
They tend to doze during buffing.
The drying coat is very popular
with these rainforest clients, applied
after a layer of verdant leaf hue.
They nod and leave at closing,
eyelids raised to sky.
Chatter later in treetops
is good for business,
even though conversation startups
sometimes take weeks for sloths.
Slow and steady, trade grows.
Nail artists vine their time.
Sloths eventually give tips.

Pineapple Beats Back Pain

When the lumbar laments lifting
one could get spinal relief
from a tiny Japanese woman's hike
up and down your bone road.
Alternative medicine dictates
that pummeling by pineapples
works as well.
Struck with maracas motion,
percussion by pineapple
can penetrate petrified muscle tissue,
promote purity
and pulverize pain.

Masai

So tall
you can measure the horizon
with your arms outstretched.
Your locks of hair are dirt-rubbed,
are bathed in blood, in urine
of the cows you cherish.

You are a warrior
of South African soil.
Beautiful in your vertical line,
perpendicular with red dust clay,
you raise your knees,
then thump earth in rhythm
with your animal and plant kin.

Spirits join in an eternal lyric,
a forever-captured air.

Masked

Almond-eyed Baule
Beaded helmet Yoruba
Baluba, Bakuba, Bambara

Oh, Oba of Ife,
this is my second face.
I am not myself.
My second face sings of ancestors.

In death, I paint white.
I honor bones,
dance memories,
beat blood drums,
balance life
and dust.

Home Again

Aye, and I saw them looking.
I didn'a bend my head.
I didn'a give them reason
to wonder. Still,
they thought the worst.
Was it my tattered dress,
my suit, my uniform?
Was it my sallow skin?
My scurvy knees?
Was it my yellowed teeth?

I'm home again.
I'm harbored
in a place long years left.
They do na' know me,
waste no talk
of my travels,
of my guard
to them—
they do na' ken
the safe I ha' brought.

So it's a pint,
and a turning
to home then, I offer,
a sleep in a still bed,
a cuppa, not a draught,
the silence of the fields,
the wind through not sails,
but oaks on the crestline,
a nightly fire on the hearth.

Hannibal

Confused, he pulled over,
looked across the busy highway,
said, "Excuse me!
Can you direct me to Highway 100 south?"

A burly man walked across,
away from his open-sided truck,
which was loaded with black
stuffed bags of who knows what.
He leaned into the open window
of our Subaru.
"You headed to Dosch?"

Short-bearded jaw, youngish,
maybe thirty-two,
he wore a red shirt,
used to be long-sleeved,
now cut and washed,
not lately but
sleeves were frayed to fuzz.
The shirt mainly covered
his beer belly.
Hair curled, snuck out
from shirt gaps of his back
and armpits.

"You gotta go down here
to those lights.
Then go more to more lights.
Then, no. That's not it.
You gotta go into town, down
there and turn.

→

Maw? They wanna go to 100.
Where's that?"

He scratched at the red shirt.
The oil stains didn't go away.
They duplicated under his fingers.

Motor running, she came across
more slowly. Mini-mother,
slight in build, grey-more-than-black
hair, long, scraggly, unwashed, unbrushed.

"We're trying to find Highway 100 south.
We're turned around. Is that way south?
It's so cloudy, we can't tell."

"You goin' to Dosch? To Bluffs?"

"We're going to Hannibal."

She finger-flicked her one front tooth,
grinned with few others, a nice woman
with warming eyes.
"We live by Hannibal. We're goin' that way.
Wanna follow us?"

"Thanks. We'll just go down here.
We'll go down to the lights.
Thanks so much. Thanks for your help."

Down the road, we pulled in
to a car mechanic's garage,
asked again, understood the path.

Finally on the right road,
our Subaru merged in behind a truck.
It took us awhile to realize
that it was laden
with black stuffed bags.
When he pulled over,
we waved thanks again
to Hannibal, in the red shirt,
giving way to us dumb elephants
motoring down the highway.

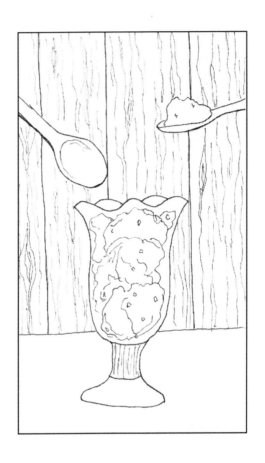

Adirondack Springtime

Red-blossom maples and lime-green,
flutter-leave locusts burst color
on the hills of upstate New York.
Fuzzy new cones appear on fir branch tips.

In a cozy, knotty pine-walled café
in upper Tupper Lake,
love blooms at the table
by the bamboo slat-shaded window.
Both in their early sixties,
they smile and titter laugh.
They rest V'd elbows,
clutch arms to shoulders,
sooth the nervousness of knees
with white cloth napkins,
furtively gaze at each other's eyes
through progressive lenses.
Savoring a shared ice cream dish
of vanilla bean,
they spoon the evening,
expand hope, linger the night.

MOMENTARY
ORDINARY

Momentary Ordinary

Soft,
the curved-edge rectangles of window
reveal a view of dark, thundering
distance between stations of Metro.
The train pummels the tunnel,
squeals the sound of bagpipe brakes
as it approaches 45th Street,
as it reaches Atlantic/Barclay, Center,
bears down on Prospect Ave.

In passing a southbound,
seconds of insight occur.
In a city of millions,
glimpses of individuals are caught
as they fly by.

A hanging head of Asian
jet-black hair bobs,
hands clutched to tattered purse.

A babushka pulled down forehead,
woman has eyes that stare only to floor.

A white-haired white man draws
with a wide-lined marker pen
in a thick, dark-covered journal.
He captures his subway subjects
without their knowledge on smooth
paper, innocent, revealing,
but in politically impolite images.
He writes entries next to them.
"If I needed money before the night

→

was done, what would I do?
If I had a gun, would it be easier
to get the money?
Question."

The girl with the strong, thick hair,
ponytailed—she with the beautiful nose,
angled sharply—she reads from a thick
book, turns the pages as the doors open
and close,
open and close.

Stand-up Mohawk blond head,
turned up t-shirt sleeve, backpack-toting
youth, student leaning towards home.
iPod buds plug his hearing the now,
give stress-relief before homework.

Small child with Hello Kitty hat
tied, not tightly under chin, smiles
at Dad, grasps hand,
hugs knee, sways with rhythm
onward to Mom.

Soft,
the curved-edge rectangles of window
reveal a view of dark, thundering
distance between stations of Metro.
In a city of forest, I am fortunate
to see the trees.

Handlin' the Pan

They would cross the street
two blocks in his advance,
walking to the 'L' train
from work at the EPA
in Chicago.

They'd spot him on Wacker
and see in his walk,
in his manner,
in his empty lunch-bag swing
a receptor,
a victim of the line,
the eye, the please sir,
that Dickens of olde used
when his Oliver wanted
more
gruel.

"Excuse me, but could you
spare a bit of change?
I haven't had a meal today.
Just a little coin, sir,
for a coffee,
if you could."

How many times had he given?
Plunked the cup,
pressed the hand,
given in,
given up?

He'd heard
many cross-the-streeters
had homes in the suburbs,
with an annual income twice his.
He'd heard the coins contributed
to the brown-bag covered,
twist-off lid
of thirst quench
gotta-have.

He'd heard of men in the Far East
who cut off a foot, a hand, two,
to look more pitiful,
to gain some metal
that they donated graciously
to the round-the-corner man,
who took it so rightfully,
who promised a good selling price
for the daughter.

Lately, he crosses the street
two blocks in advance
and deaf-ears the shouts
of the begging voice and the 'L' train
to deposit the retained money
in the slide-out arm
of his bank's automatic teller.

Corner of 3rd and Magnolia

The tall pin-striped man with the purple umbrella
pulled the cord.
The bus stopped.
He got off.

A short lady with black hair twisted up
in a rhinestone clip
got on carrying a mesh green bag.

On the corner, a long necked, sooty-colored mouse
periscoped the road from the curb,
then dashed, corgi-like,
across two, three lanes of vehicles
before becoming a large macadam gumlump
at the corner of 3rd and Magnolia.

An Ed's Drywall truck had weighted its turn
with 1.4 tons of 5/8 inch.

The bus, innocent, collected fare
and proceeded to Catalpa.

Little Italy

She walked the west side
of the street, cool to the glances
of stone buildings.
Dark hair curtained her face.
Magnetic eyes of passersby
willed her to look up.
She gazed only at the concrete,
sight-sweeping the sidewalk
for the silver earring
she'd lost this way
the morning of her first communion.
How many years ago,
how many parish wafers was it now?
That earring long gone
to another, larger ear.

Gaining a Seat on the R

I swung on to an already full-train,
was lucky to spot a seat,
next to you.
I hand-circled down the grasp pole,
sat on the edge of your knitted red scarf.

My thigh knew it didn't belong there.
You knew, too.
Edging the last row of purl,
I quickly yielded inches of space.
It was a nice scarf, bright in color.

You tugged quietly, politely,
not even turning your head
or your eyes,
as if my move was your mistake.

I recognized a cable in the pattern,
wanted to ask you, wanted to tell you.
Do you knit? Did you make it?
It's a beautiful scarf.

But I am from the Midwest.
I'm a tourist.
I don't know the ways of silence,
of no conversation,
even when there is an opening.

I stared across the aisle at thumbs
rhythmically hitchhiking iPhones,
consulting apps, playing games.
What a waste, I thought.

$\longrightarrow$

Here are neighbors, potential
friends in the flesh, and all they want
for conversation,
for interaction,
is a digital metal companion.

The scarf got up and left the car,
trained in quiet unobtrusive ways.
I watched the blackness in the windows
speed by.

Music in the City

For Tamara and Mike

Listen! Can you hear it?
There is music in the city.
There's a hum.
There's a beat.
There's a metro melody

in the clatter-race up/down
subway stairs to cross-town.
There's a steely guitar glide
in a metro card slide.
There's a long-winded whine
in the turnstile line.
There is music to wake up to
in the squeal of the brakes
rounding tunnel turns
to your stop.

There's the count at each corner
by the white man walking:
14, 13, 12, 11...4, 3, 2—
and you run the white-lined safe path
to beat the red hand halting,
or you don't, and they don't
wave, but timpani-beat their fists
out car windows.

Shrill trumpet sirens accost your ears,
weave their theme from pianissimo to forte
as their vehicles knit the traffic lanes
seeking the quiet coda of a hospital zone.

Sherlock Holming-pigeons flap and eye,
strut and sputter, puff and peck.
Always busy, always muttering,
so that the unsuspecting never realize
their coos are clues deciphered.

The slap-clap of the pedestrian smack
on the city cab,
that dares trespass on a walker,
is not applause.
The words that follow are blue, not blues,
but jazz the day for those in earshot.

Romanian, Spanish, Irish, French,
Jamaican, German, Italian, and Polish
form language chords of harmony,
sometimes cacophony,
on sidewalks where sales are friendly
but insistent.

Fountains splash.
Trees wind-murmur.
Dogs yelp and croon.
Cats sing romantic meows
to birds, who know better
than to stay and listen
on fire-escape fences.

Listen! Can you hear it?
There is music in the city.
There's a hum.
There's a beat.

→

There's a metro melody.
Even in the night,
it snores a symphony,
dreams a waltz of waking.

Rats in D.C.

Robust and Reginald Rat ran a realty business
under the ivy in Adams Morgan,
just off the red line in D.C.
Rob and Reggie, for short, were short.
They were big-haunched rodents.

Their office was directly beneath the window
of a garden apartment on Ontario Street.
They located there
because they liked the sound of that name.
It had a foreign, sophisticated ring to it:
Ontario.

The yards, if you could call them that,
were 8' x 8', sloped down to cement.
Prospective customers eyed the space,
questioned their lot.

Rob would say, "This is superbia.
This is the front yard. Look at the overhang
of this magnificent ivy!
Who could want for more privacy?"

Reggie would take them out back
by the garbage cans, the dumpsters.
"You wouldn't have to live here,
with this stench, with the riffraff,
but you would have complete access here,
come and go as you pleased.
It would be a strip mall to you,
easy for take-away, convenient for cruising."

It was the swishing sound
under the big starry-shaped ivy leaves
that sold them.
They bought in to the residential rat ranches.
No high rises here—
only single tunnel, lateral homes,
spread out in the shade of green ivy.

Friendly neighbors, busy neighbors,
who were always intent on healthy practices
of speed walking, of calorie counting,
greeted them at the curb in late night encounters.

The young woman who lived in the garden apartment—
her only window, the one beneath
which the realty office was housed,
heard the rustle of the night breeze,
breathed in the ivy air,
dreamed of the gym, where next day
she would treadmill
while dark green fan blades circled her head.

Racing the Heat Wave

Up on the step,
her toes curl, brace.
Bending forward,
she dives
into the first heat
of the race.

Her hair spreads
     in zigzag fans.
          Her arms paddle,
               stirring the moist.

Forward thrusting,
     energy pooled,
          she gains yards
               of distance.

Water beads her brow.
     Water beads her arms.
          It rolls in rivers down
               her neck, her back.
                    Her legs glisten.

Almost to the goal,
     almost to the finish,
          her sandals slip.

Her St. Christopher medal
               sticks to her chest.

She gains the car door,
     slips inside,
          turns the key,
               wins the prize:

                    the cool of the AC.

Rush to Win

Must be postmarked by midnight, April 29th.
You could be a winner of a Million Dollars!
It's easy. Just check box number one,
add a stamp and mail!
And you get the magazines.
What a deal! It's the deal of a lifetime!
Think of it! You, a Millionaire!
What could you do with a Million Dollars?!

A new house in the suburbs
instead of that downtown cardboard lean-to,
atop the airflow grate on Rush St.

A new car rather than that Safeway shopping cart,
complete with black, mostly-filled-with-air bags
and those no lace, hole-ridden Nikes
two sizes too big.

Health insurance, for visits with smiles
and respect as a benefitted, card-carrying member
instead of found, frayed sweaters,
public toilet paper-wrapped wounds,
and earth-smeared salve of life on bedbug bites.

A Diner's Club Card instead of a diving dumpster dash,
leftover lo mein, lasagna on the fly, limburger
on plastic wrap, Styrofoam, cardboard insert.

A bank account with checking on checking
and savings on savings,
no fees in your interest,
no stooping for pennies,
no asking for quarters,
no pleading the fifth for a fifth
to ease the pain
of no coin, no abode,
no car, no Band-Aid,
no food,

no stamp.

In Chicago

garbage trucks eat Honda Civics
for breakfast

weed gangs, descendants of seedy offshoots,
form military lines in city sidewalk's crack

cocaine is sold over the counter, under
the viaduct, down on the corner, cross town

old souped-up flatties
insist megaphonically the earth
is doomed and Jesus is coming

asphalt salves the holey pavement

women in public toilet stalls
brace themselves, like track sprinters
without blocks, to avoid beaded porcelain

half-eaten Bismarck, raspberry
filling, gels in ceramic-tiled cubbyhole
on subway stairs waiting
for a return chew or sharing

the 'L', squealing greasily,
races overhead,
conductor nasally garbling,
"Armitage…Armitage will be next…Armitage…"

WHAT
NANA KNOWS

Trick or Treat

First a mouse came to my door,
then a duck,
next a dog demanding treats,
followed by an elephant.
A parade of animals
all ringing the bell
in the late fall sunshine.

Almost done with saving time,
I was not done with saving chocolate.
I said to the dog, "You can't have chocolate.
It will kill you."
He protested that he was a strong dog,
a wise dog, could even take
chocolate through an IV, if need be,
and need there was.
He muzzle-nuzzled me for a Nestlé.

Halloween, a time of year, a time of mind,
when serotonin levels swell
at just the thought of candy.
Sugar keeps those little legs pumping,
down streets, up steps, over sidewalk cracks.
Lights on porches draw them in like moths.
Some are reluctant to say the magic words.
Some are brash and grab their own choice
from the bowels of the bowl.
They turn, after three small words,
stumble down to mothers,
fall into waiting strollers
pushed by fathers, who extract their toll
with a snicker, to the next yard.

A Winter Walk to School

With mouths recently warmed
by breakfast chocolate,
children suck stalactite ice
on the way to St. Mary's.

Snapped from windowsills by backdoors
they clutch the clear tapered teeth
like mass candles.

The procession of mittened hands
moves slowly past driveway pews.
Loose boots clunk the snow-packed aisles.

Heavy packs thump
their puffy-mantled backs
and cold breaths of diluted cocoa-smoke
incense the matin air.
Snow pants whine liturgically.

As December school bells chime
icicle stubs are cast down.
Catechism calls.
Daily sentences need Sister's correction.

Reform

She knew she shouldn't have done it—snuck out of bed in the dark hours before dawn.

Down the stairs she tiptoed, her right hand feeling the wall all the way to the living room.

There, the street lamp provided a crack of light through the mostly closed curtains.

She crawled her way to the end table by the couch, where she had left her Easter basket with the barren green shreddy grass.

She was delighted to find it now full. The bunny had delivered and hopped out.

There was a huge chocolate rabbit. She couldn't resist, ate both ears right down to his brunette skull.

Her mother would be so upset, just as she was at Christmas, when all the packages were unwrapped while still in the closet—even the ones she'd found under the guest room bed.

She knew she could make things right if she could just get the bag of Nestlé Morsels from the third shelf of the kitchen cupboard, melt them in her hand.

She would reform.

She knew she could.

Raspberry Revelations

Emmaline did not know
there were creatures
in her mother's garden.
She didn't know their look,
their voice, their odd dance.

One morning, upon awakening
early, hungry, she ventured out,
her binkie trailing the mulch path
to the raspberry patch.
Under curved bough, prickle stem,
hang-swinging on ripe berry-hold
she saw them.

"Oh, my!" the wee, foot-tall girly one
with the chin dimple, cried.
The red-violet stain on her bodice
gave away her guilt of thievery.

"It's a good thing we came up early
for here's another one after our breakfast!
Isn't it enough that we have to contend
with sparrows and a furry gold-dog puppy?"

A boy creature, smelling the sweet, ripe
grabbed the wee one's legs.
"Aye," he voiced in a bellow.
"It's past our sun time, girl!
We must dance and go now.
Fair game to the pup who sits
and chooses the ripest to seine
through young teeth."

And dance, he did, swiveling
the canes, hop-popping
the lazy unripe,
admonishing them for lazy, slow.
Sun day hours bring the reckoning.

Emmaline wrapped binkie to shoulders,
chose carefully the leftovers,
thought long and hard about raspberry revelations.

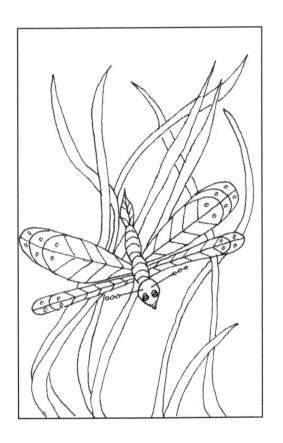

Camatagliora

Fifteen-year-old Adley sat cross-legged in the grass of her backyard. She was supposed to be mowing but had run it out of gas.

Catching her breath, she was picking short green cuts off her now dyed shoes, when she saw a tiny movement to the left of her shoelace.

Not sure she'd actually seen something, she stared in concentration at a two-foot diameter area of lawn-growth.

Ah, there it was again. But what was it? Iridescent purple wings flattened to a black segmented body, six spindly legs, yellow eyes lidded in red, outlined in black—what a look, she thought. "Stunning!"

"Who are you?" she asked, remembering the Cheshire Cat from Wonderland.

The insect gazed at Adley and, without a word, sent the word *Camatagliora* to her consciousness.

"Where do you come from?" thought Adley, and again the word *Camatagliora* became known.

"Adley! Can you please finish mowing? It's almost supper," her dad shouted from the back porch.

Slowly to feet, she scooped up Camatagliora, put him on a bobbing fern, well away from the rotating blades.

Yellow eyes, lidded in red, outlined in black followed her.

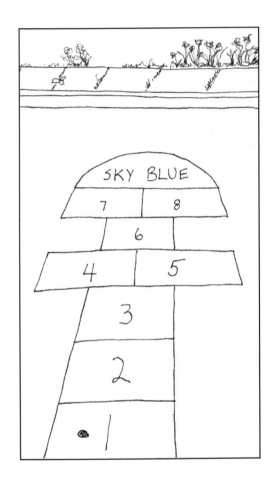

98

Faith in Hopscotch

Mary Louise threw the pebble.
It landed in the square of 1.
She hopped over
that real estate of being
to 2, and beyond,
past the earth,
into the firmament,
and back.

She proceeded to the box of 2,
of 3, the crossroads of 4, 5:
purgatory, the priests said it was.
She wanted only to play
this game, hopscotch,
with the other children on the block.

To rest at Sky Blue was heaven,
a pause in paradise before traversing
the levels of sin to get back home.

Grasping that little piece of rock,
Mary Louise maneuvered back
through ancient realms of time,
scratching the unknown.
With faith in balance, she traversed life—
no explanations necessary.
Confident in her passage,
she released the stone to 6.

Breakfast at 4 and 2

Glistening brunette bangs, sheared
to level-float the glycerin bead,
and eyebrow fences, parallel, an inch below,
guard globe eyes of grey-green.
Rimmed with lashes, they blink-whip
joyful surprise at the present of a waffle,
mountain-peaked with cream.

How quickly, though,
do eyebrows middle-plunge to V's,
like drawn-in-flight birds skying afar.
The downturned scowl repeats
in pout lips, the bottom puffed out pinkly,
when mother presses juice first.

With an "ick," an "uh-uhn,"
and a bobble of shoulder,
the creamed screen, syrup now added,
moves farther away down the table,
as grapefruit liquid advances forward.

Silent, sodium tears round cheek-curves to chin.
Stiff, crossed arms are elbow-released.
Small sisters' sips are rewarded
with sweet repast.

Summer Winter Weave

Mother, I am so cold!
Pull the cover up, Son. It will warm you.
It's made of woolsy, our lambs' love
sheared, combed, spun.
You started the great wheel.
You kept it turning while I
captured fiber fleece
to weave a winter welcome
for your night dreams.

Mother, I am so warm!
Push the cover off. You need it not.
Summer linsey's light can weight
on this starry night in August
when heat-sleep escapes
and down to the river
you run
for a midnight dip
in blanketed darkness.

Unicorn

Until she was fourteen,
nightly, she would prepare for the visit,
insulate a corner of her room for him
with curtains, push-pinned to the ceiling,
on the chance that while she was half-asleep
rainbows of light might burst from his hiding place,
negating his power should her eyes catch the colors.

Silent Picture Show

In the sky, a dragon opens his mouth,
sprays white fire on a bunny's
Belgian endive ears.
Puffs of cauliflower drift
from the blue hors d'oeuvres platter
to hide within a baseball mitt.

Albino crows silently caution
baby seals about murder.
Snowy mountain masses merge.
No rocks are up thrown.
No faults are accused.

I close my eyes.
Under the dark dome behind lids,
mind-clouds commence
a double feature.

Where Wagons Go

Do you have a wagon?
Do you know where it wants to go?
Do you have gills?
Do you know where gills can take you?

Sometimes Mom gives me a box.
She gives me crayons.
I draw wheels.
She says, "Play."
I pull the box.
It's a wagon.
It goes where it wants.
Then it stops.
I play there.

It's a place, underwater.
The wheels sink.
The sand is soft.
I use the crayons to dig holes.

Crayfish, relatives of crayons,
come out.
They don't have gills.
They like the wagon.
They pinch-claw at the wheels
and stare at the lug nuts.
They think it's snack time.

I like the wagon, too.
It goes places.
It goes to my places.
I see crayfish.
I see Seaweedia,
the princess of the ocean.

She has gills.
She helps me by putting
her finger in my nose.
She pulls me through the currents.
Mom wouldn't approve.
She'd like it, though,
that I can breathe that way.

Do you have a wagon?
Do you know where it wants to go?
Do you have gills?
Do you know where gills can take you?

Sometimes I just go.
Sometimes it's better that way.
You should try it.
You could come with me.
It would be fun.

Great White Night Shark

"Wanna jump off the pier?" he said,
"They're all in bed, asleep.
We could go. We could do it.
The great white night shark
might be out, but maybe not.
We could chance it.
Wanna?"

What? Wanna?
I'm his cousin.
I'm three years younger.
He has armpit hair.
He has a six pack muscle chest.
Like I'm gonna refuse
this invite?

The sky is the only part
of the world that's quiet.
Cicadas chirp. Frogs sing harmony.
Wind ruffles tree skirts.
Planets are silent—stars, too.
I haven't learned how
to manipulate girls
with those night shiners yet.

The lake water looks black,
like spooky midnight
horror-show glass,
with Svengooli's face
popping up suddenly to freak me out
of my "falling asleep" mode.

We dive: me first, him after.
The water is cold, late July cold
in these northern Wisconsin parts.
He goes under fast, real fast,
doesn't come up, doesn't surface.
I look around, turn circles,
see the moon rotate with me
on the black glass.
I look for his face ascending,
see only Svengooli.

Suddenly, I feel something grip my leg,
tug me down. I panic.
It's the great white night shark!
I can't let it get me, like it got him.
I have to get back, get to the pier.
I pull, stroke. The power
of my arms amazes me.
We rise, in unison, my cousin and me.
I'm left clutching the ladder,
hoisting my leg to solid rung.
He sputters, "Did you see him?"
I see teeth marks on my ankle.
I crawl to bunk
but I don't sleep that night.

Cartwheels

She turns cartwheels on the boardwalk
of the Harbour Front Centre in Toronto.
Bagpipes bray the nearby stage
for dancers in plaid kilt competition.

Hand down, leg up.
Hand down, leg up.

Circling over straight legged,
toes pointed, arms taut, back flat,
she spins the breeze of the bay
again and again.

I think bucket list,
remember Chicago sidewalk air-turns,
feel the dizziness upon standing,
long for it again.

My arms would crack bones at the weight.
My back would flail.
My right-angle feet would droop like lead
and haul my calves and thighs with them.
I'd land as a lump of bruise and scrape,
with a firm belief in gravity.

Best just to watch her.

At Elkhart Lake

Wind wrinkles water,
matching the dry, brown skin
on my suntanned arm.

My hand holds tight the gunnels
as we slap-wake the afternoon
boating on Elkhart Lake.

Tree silhouettes hover at lake edges.
Brightly colored chairs line piers.
Laughter of children diving,
jumping from school to summer,
echo-bounce wave to wave.
Lonely rafts, tethered to rock bottom,
wait for weekend loungers.

Overstuffed bikini-women nurse
gin and tonics with lime,
watch toddlers and shih tzus.
Pontoons are crowded with visitors
bound for float-motor excursions.

A small boy at the boat landing
caresses a caught sunnie,
smoothes his left hand down
from gasping mouth past gills.
Holding steady, he curves the hook
from lip, tosses life back.
He sits then, lake-swishes his bare feet,
waits for toe nibbles.

What Nana Knows

In the shadows of the dog house
on the third floor in the nursery,
silent signals meet
with canine conscience.
Slurpy drools dictate lessons,
shadows of puppy youth.
Kind, curly blankets of fur,
hairy handfuls in fond fists,
the fuzz is not in Nana's head.
She sees the night sky
from the dark of a quiet window.
She counts the stars
that pattern picture stories.
She knows she's too fat to fly.
Warming the sill, she jolts in dreams,
waking to want realities
of her darling children.
Adventures in lands never to be seen,
Nana knows the shadows,
tinkers with time, and waits.

A STRANGE TRANSPORT

A Strange Transport

Sitting in the audience, midway,
right center, seat 9,
I was engaged by the performance
to this point.
He came down into our midst,
looking, seeking a participant,
for the next intrigue.

He paused in front of me,
extended from his hand a ticket.
No blisters there, I noted,
coming from farming stock.

I took his offering,
was led onstage,
was led to believe in mystery,
in magic.

The box was wooden.
The box was narrow.
The box was long.
I fit into it though 5' 10".
Reclining felt good.
I was part of a trick.

The box lid closed,
to music, soft, relaxing,
and I hummed along,
shutting my eyes.

A question came to my brain
minutes later.
When does he open the box?
When do I sit up?
When do I climb out to applause?

Blackness came then,
a tunneling down,
swift and sure and steady.
Time became still.
Time became…
Time relinquished becoming.
Time was gone.

I was still.
Not here.
Not there.
What is this?
Where is this?

Is all the world a stage
until the end of Act III?
Who writes the final lines?
Who writes the epilogue?

Is the passage from here
to there
so easy?
Why did I need a ticket
for such a strange transport?

True Grit

When one sieves sand,
each grain yields a view
of its shielded sedimentary sides.
Sand stubbornly sticks in the screen,
just as it stubbornly rolls and tosses,
wave after tumbling wave.

In close examination, twelve grains
are not better than one.
Unique as a winter's snowflake,
each deserves scrutiny.
With eye rappelling down its shiny face,
the mind recalls past journeys of ions,
of eons of time.

Sand is hem-trapped in the coat of many colors,
thrown upward by Cleopatra's dancing,
toe-ringed foot.
It is the skin chafer of posing Polynesians
in Gauguin paintings of Tahitian tints.
Sand is the firm boot grip on Normandy shore,
the on-holiday, head-out burial at Brighton Beach.
Sand layers the glass, makes the glass jar
show its flickering facets in candlelight glimmer.

A Fourth for Bridge

Paddling along,
a neophyte to swimming,
I flailed arms and legs.
After a full comida of fish tacos
at an outdoor café in Lima,
my overstuffed belly hung down
in the salted, tepid water.
It tempted the Leviathan melvillei.

That powerful creature below me
rose up for its meal.
In an open-mouthed *shlup*,
I was swallowed.
The ancient sperm whale,
content for the moment,
oared fins to the deep.

I waterslid down his throat to the party.
A warm group of three greeted me:
Jonah, Captain Ahab, and a little Inuit man
named Aukaneck.

"We don't know why he can't control him!"
the first two exclaimed of the third.
"He could do it if he tried.
He told us Aukaneck means
god of whale movement."

"He who remains nameless
wouldn't like it," Jonah cried.
"Oh, whale, you devil incarnate," spat Ahab.

Aukaneck eyed them calmly,
offered me a slimy seat,
took cards out of his seal coat pocket,
told me I was South, his partner.
"Let's play," he said.
"We've been waiting for you."

Iditarod

Come to me awake in the black seal
of night sleep,
when the unquenchable wind
howls,
when the silver whistle is raised
to stiff-skin lips,
and giant paws are summoned.

Bounding they come, leaping,
teething the cold,
biting the air,
rolling and tumbling
in the anxiety of delight.

Pile under the blankets.
Await the word:
"Mush!"
that sends us at dawn
to the unhorizon
of white.

To Concede

After awhile the needle pokes easily,
a thin sliver in vein.

After awhile the craving pain subsides.

Incoherent ravings submit to quivers.

Ears hear the hum of the universe
as it swells through fluid-saturated mists.

Skin levitates white cotton coolness.

The body cradles its spindly limbs
close to trunk.

It teeters, rocks,
like an egg
whose yolk is pulled, as if by magnet,
towards middle earth,
suspended in calm.

Stone Angel

It's hard trying to become—
perfect.

My being tips grey the day's light.
My wings are heavy.

I lean forward,
bend my knees,
brace my left foot,
heel my dress.

I "W" my arms
to catch world-first elbows
when I fall.

My eyes seek,
my neck strains for guidance.

My finger-touch hands grasp life air.
It tunnels through, swirls back
to feathers, to grasses, to leaves.

It's hard trying to become—
perfect.

Death Row Gift

I will make you a wall of color:
a painters' chip wall of hues and tones and shades,
that you may not think about the shades
and the river and Charon, but be calmed.

Pick a color, any color.
What does it make you think of?

Blue of the sea you never got to see, the sky, the robin's birth egg,
the bedspread of your grandmother,
your Cookie Monster cup of kid-dom from Goodwill.

Green of the beret-soldier figures you played in the alley with
your one friend, Sam,
shot in the lung by a drive-by.
Green of the refrigerator leftovers and, yes, the refrigerator
itself.
Green of the few weeds struggling to survive the shoe treads in
the cracks of the
sidewalk outside.

Yellow of the sun, of the heat of the 3rd floor walkup in the
summer with the no AC
and the no ice and the no water,
of the no money for the bill.

Yellow of the father who walked in swagger.
Read: fled in fear of the responsibility, of the work to provide for
a family,
a son: you.

Red of the small valentine given in 3rd grade by a teacher who
cared,
Mrs. Simon.

Red of the car—the Mustang—stolen
from the 7-Eleven parking lot that night.

Red of the flush of your cheek as the accelerator pushed on
down.

Red of the stop sign that was missed.

Red of the lights spinning in the mirror—rear view—look back.
Looking back now too late.

Red of the blood that spurted from the cop's head as you
panicked.

Red of that jury woman's blouse.

Black of the straps and the blindfold to come.

Blue of the sea, of the sky, of the robin's birth egg,
of Gran's bedspread to finger, to bunch, to hug.

Blue of the breath seen foggy in the cold
on the corner watching white light above.

Card Wars

Weapons had been dealt,
troops arranged,
battles contemplated
across the felt of the field.
Three kings stood the edge of the crowd:
two bachelors and one with a wife—
a wife with a big heart.
Their sons were a handful,
had left them for another side,
for other games of adventure.
The three kings were wise.
They stood in solidarity
away from their motley assortment
of penny ante militia.
Hopeful in their strength,
They failed to realize
that three stiff Cyclopses,
those one-eyed monsters,
could defeat them,
slam their power,
force the kings to shuffle away.

A Curious Alien Visit

Long after your curtains meet
at window's middle,
after bolts are thrown,
and quilts are drawn up to chin,
in the security of night, you sleep.
Outside, under your foreign moon
and my one familiar star,
wind flutters the scales on my right appendage.
It lifts their luminescent edges,
mica-like, reflecting this sky circle's light.
Alone, I halt my procured vehicle at ridge peak,
hold steady to a gravel path
with the clawed points of my three toes.
An old bike—no shoe clips,
as on the one I couldn't ride—
only hard rubber palettes to press forward.
No click, click, spin return,
just silent pressure stop.
I calculate the simple distance/rate/time
from peak to shoreline
by this bike, by flight,
take into account breeze velocity
of minutes/seconds.
My purple facetted eyes readjust the landscape:
a kaleidoscope of dark tree lines,
feather-edged foliage, geometric solid structures.
I hear many human heartbeats,
and the low rhythm of night-breath in your town.
Wind flutters the scales on my right appendage.
In seconds, they flatten to your earth's wet element
as I dive, swordlike, deeper.

Roundabout

For Patty Aker

Blue, so blue it stains
the lips of your brain,
a hurricane sea swoops the swells,
pinepitches a ship onto shoals,
swallows crows' nest,
stills wailing tongues, teeth, taut line
roundabout 1624.
Neither reefed sails
nor looped bowlen help
in the eye of doomstorm.

Warm the water,
so brim-rimming with salt,
it grains fingerprints from digits.
Pirate bones add calcium to coral.
Berths add birthing rooms
for big-eye angels, gars, and barracudas.
Rays pass swiftly,
maneuvering their magic-carpet bodies,
blanketing the bottom-shine treasure.

Circles upon circles,
upon circles –
underwater orbs
reflect Apollo rains.
Apollo reigns,
dropping gold rounds—
spattercoins to the blue,
so blue it stains the lips
of your brain.

The Bridges at Corpus Callosum

I was drinking coffee in the kitchen yesterday morning
when a three legged monkey on wooden-spoon crutches
ambled in to chat.

He spoke to me of many things:
of vine flights through lost mind jungles
and hardships he suffered there.
The overgrowth of vegetation
had kept him battling for years.
"List plants, creeping to-doos,
boxkeeper squash greens," he called them.

While traversing the lowest beam of a bent-
over statusquo tree, he had slipped.
His leg was swallowed by a hollow.
It was six months before his stump healed.

Regaining strength, he looked around
with a new sparkle in his left eye,
tore branches from the tree,
fashioned his crutches.

Stubbornly and ever onward,
he skip-plodded until at last he saw bridges.
They were swinging bridges made of rope-like tendrils.

Approaching, he knew they were strong and secure.
They seemed to have been used repeatedly.
So he crossed, sensing old, but somehow familiar, longings.

There, on the other side, he felt at home.
There were his dreammates, his family, whole and intact.
They welcomed him with a feast of unlimited proportion,
hummed melodies he'd forgotten, but now recognized.

I asked him, "Why have you come to me?"

"Your journey is over now, too," he replied. "You're home.
Welcome and be happy."

I gave him coffee and borrowed his spoon to stir.

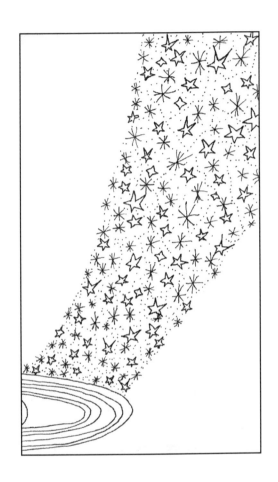

Walking to Saturn

It would be a lot of work
to walk to Saturn,
if you could walk to Saturn.
Millions of miles
with a heavy pack,
pushing planets off your back,
stars ringing in your ears,
dancing in circles,
gone light years.

It would be a lot of work
hiking there and back
to retell night stories
first told by the big guy:
Jupiter, the main man,
red-faced at Mars' indiscretion—
but we won't talk about that.
What happens in black holes
stays in black holes.

When I was little, my mother walked my sister, brother, and me to the library every week. We brought home bag-loads of books. I liked the pictures in books the best because I read the stories visually. Cozied in the bathtub with my blanket and pillow, that's where I learned to read.

Dad would recite Longfellow's "This is the forest primeval, the murmuring pines and the hemlocks, bearded in moss and in garments green, indistinct in the twilight."

Fairy tales were "indistinct." Dick, Jane, Sally, and Puff were not. I learned to make up my own stories and started writing them down as poems when I was thirteen. Before that time, I drew pictures of them.

I was born in Chicago, a big city by a lake. We followed the lake north to Highland Park, where I completed middle and high school. I studied at Ohio Wesleyan University and graduated in art education from University of Wisconsin-Madison.

Lake Michigan, my first sea because I could not see across it, led me to a study program aboard a ship: a semester at sea, which took me to many ports. It both broadened and condensed my world, showed me sameness and diversity. I gathered visual stories in abundance.

Observations of people, places, and events figure prominently in my free verse. Some observations are factual, some created from imagination. I believe both have merit, with those from imagination having a greater say. When we stop imagining, we lose the ability to go forward, to create. We get stuck in a history box of another's creation. Our world needs to give credence to innovators, imaginers. From them, wonder can be realized.

Marilyn Zelke-Windau

36756883R00082

Made in the USA
Charleston, SC
18 December 2014